VENTURING THE DEEP SEA

LAURIE LINDOP

Twenty-First Century Books
Minneapolis

Dedicated to
Captain Karen Luknis and
Captain Debra Butler

Front cover photograph courtesy of OAR/National Undersea Research Program (NURP); University of Hawaii (photographer T. Kerby).

Photographs courtesy of © Gene Carl Feldman: pp. 4, 11; Harbor Branch: pp. 8 (Wes Skiles), 14 (Edith Widder), 57 (Mark Schrope); © Edith Widder/HBOI/Visuals Unlimited: p. 15; © Bettmann/CORBIS: pp. 19, 20, 23; U. S. Naval Historical Center: p. 24; Office of Naval Research: pp. 26, 34; © Emory Kristoff/NGS Image Collection: pp. 35, 36; © Ralph White/CORBIS: pp. 39, 42; Woods Hole Oceanographic Institution: pp. 40, 46, 50 (E. Paul Oberlander); William R. Normark/USGS: p. 48; © Roger Ressmeyer/CORBIS: p. 53 (both); Sea Studios: pp. 54, 55; OAR/National Undersea Research Program (NURP): p. 56; © Jonathan Blair/CORBIS: p. 59 (top); © 2003 MBARI: pp. 59 (bottom), 60; © 1998 Commander Submarine Force, U. S. Pacific Fleet: pp. 64, 66, 68

Illustrations by Ron Miller

Twenty-First Century Books
A division of Lerner Publishing Group
241 First Avenue North
Minneapolis, Minnesota 55401 U.S.A.

Website address: www.lernerbooks.com

Library of Congress Cataloging-in-Publication Data
Lindop, Laurie.
Venturing the deep sea / by Laurie Lindop.
p. cm. — (Science on the edge)
Includes bibliographical references and index.
ISBN-13: 978-0-7613-2701-1 (lib. bdg. : alk. paper)
ISBN-10: 0-7613-2701-0 (lib. bdg. : alk. paper)
1. Submarine topography—Juvenile literature.
2. Deep sea ecology—Juvenile literature.   I. Title.
GC83.L45 2006
551.46—dc22   2004029729

Manufactured in the United States of America
1 2 3 4 5 6 – DP – 10 09 08 07 06

CONTENTS

Dr. Clyde Roper hoses off a giant squid that was caught dead in a fishing trawl around the waters of New Zealand.

INTRODUCTION

Meet a Deep-Sea Scientist

Zoologist Dr. Clyde Roper loves squid. He loves to eat squid; he loves to study squid. He's got tens of thousands of squid specimens floating in jars at his Washington, D.C., lab. At home, he's got squid art, squid coffee cups, squid windsocks, squid kites, squid neckties. Rolling up his sleeves and pulling up a pant leg, he'll show you squid scars from his near-fatal encounter with the ferocious Humboldt variety.

There's one particular squid, above all others, that obsesses this scientist: the giant deep-sea squid. "Oh, it's a gorgeous, beautiful animal," rhapsodizes Roper.[1] But so far, he's seen only dead ones. No human has ever laid eyes on a giant squid in its natural environment. We know they exist only because dead ones periodically wash ashore or get hauled up in fishing nets.

5

Even lying lifeless on a beach, a giant deep-sea squid is an awesome creature. It grows to the length of two school buses and has volleyball-sized eyes, eight arms covered with suction cups, and two whiplike tentacles to bring food (either fish or smaller squid) to its powerful parrotlike beak. It tears this food to bits and sucks it down its throat, which, oddly enough, runs straight through its highly developed brain.

It would seem that something so massive would be easy to find, but giant squid live in the single most unexplored environment on Earth, the deep ocean. Swimming at depths of about 2,300 to 4,500 feet (700 to 1,372 meters), these squid make their home in a region far below where sunlight can penetrate. Only recently have submersibles (research submarines) been developed that are capable of making the journey down to these extreme depths.

Yet, some researchers think it's pointless to even try to find a squid using a submersible. Roper admits, "If you spent a day hunting in a sub, you'd think you're covering a lot of territory, but relative to the amount of water in the ocean, you're really not."[2] On top of that, a sub sends out glaring lights that would likely startle a giant squid. Or maybe make it mad enough to attack. No one really knows.

"We probably know more about the dinosaurs than about the giant squid," says Roper. "And that's what lures me on. I don't have to find the biggest. I just want to find where they live, what they do down there, how they move, how they mate."[3] If he could just see a minute or two of squid video footage, he'd learn volumes. The problem, however, is getting that video footage.

Roper came up with a brainstorm. Instead of going down into the deep sea in a sub himself, he'd send an emissary on his behalf: the sperm whale. These whales are the only creatures big enough to eat giant squid, which apparently they do with relish. The indigestible squid beaks have been found in their stomachs, and sperm whales sometimes sport massive tentacle scars. Roper's plan was to attach video cameras to sperm whales so they could become unwitting filmmakers. "When the sperm whale starts to hunt, we'll be following," said Roper.[4]

In 1996, he headed for a site in the Azores, off the coast of Portugal, where numerous dead squid had been sighted and sperm whales congregated. From aboard a research ship, he and his crew scanned the sun-splashed waves looking for whales. Whenever they saw one, they'd climb into inflatable kayaks and paddle toward it. Their flimsy kayaks would rise and fall on the waves as they approached the creature. If they made it to within arm's length, they leaned over and attempted to stick the "crittercam" onto the whale with a big suction cup.

"It was not an easy thing to do," Roper acknowledged. "Often we would get two arm's lengths away and the whale would dive."[5] In all, they managed to stick crittercams on twelve whales, and they gathered amazing footage. Here was the ocean from the whale's point of view: a rush of greenish blue as the whale dove downward, embarking on a roller coaster ride of effortless propulsion. One whale captured footage of a row of sleeping whales floating vertically, like pickets in a fence. Roper waited for the moment when he'd see a squid's massive eyeball focusing in on the crittercam as the whale prepared to attack. But no such luck.

The whales dove and frolicked and went about their lives, but they did not hunt squid on camera. Nonetheless, Roper judged the expedition a tremendous success in terms of information gathered about sperm whales. Since then, he's gone on other squid safaris, but his beloved remains elusive. Ever the optimist, Roper asserts, "This is part of a much bigger quest. It is not about instant gratification. It is exciting that there are still these mysteries to be probed and explored."[6]

Scientists estimate that humans have investigated at most 1 percent of the deep sea.

CHAPTER ONE

The Unknown Deep

In our modern world, it may seem like there are no new places to discover, no chance to venture into uncharted territory. In fact, between the surface of the sea and the ocean floor, there lies a largely unexplored realm. "The ocean is home to the greatest diversity on the planet," said oceanographer Dr. Sylvia Earle. "It's still ironic that there are more footprints on the moon than there are on the bottom of the sea."[1]

When scientists take the plunge down to our ocean's farthest depths, they often find that neither their book learning nor their imagination has prepared them for what they encounter. Diving in tiny submersibles, they see thousands of never-before-cataloged creatures floating past their portholes, many glowing with their own light. When they reach the seafloor, scientists train their lights on a barren world where underwater mountains soar higher than Mt. Everest and trenches plunge deeper than the Grand Canyon. They witness scenes of fresh geological violence in which the surface of the Earth has split apart and molten rock has poured out.

The deep sea is a vast place, and not surprisingly, the scientists studying it have a variety of specialties—too many to list. In general, they seek to answer questions such as: How many creatures live in the deep sea? What do they look like, how do they interact, and what strategies do they use to survive in an environment so different from our own? How is underwater terrain different from surface terrain? What chemical, environmental, or geological forces shape the deep sea?

Most research takes place in labs rather than underwater. It's expensive to use submersibles. To get funding, scientists must prove to universities or oceanographic institutions that making the trip underwater is the only possible way to further their studies and acquire the information they need. Equally important, they must convince other scientists that such a venture will likely yield significant scientific rewards that can then be shared through the whole scientific community. If they finally get the opportunity to venture underwater, scientists must then go back into their labs and spend months, even years, cataloging and studying the specimens and data they've collected. If necessary, they may, at a later date, apply to take another trip down.

This book focuses on that exciting moment when a deep-sea biologist or geologist gets ready to board a submersible and embark on a cutting-edge expedition. You will join the scientists as the submersible's door is sealed shut and they start to sink down toward an unknown world full of both unexpected marvels and unforeseen hazards. You will also learn about some of the visionary pioneers who made the deep sea accessible by con-

Deep-sea scientists spend a lot of time in their labs studying the specimens and data they've collected.

structing diving machines. Entrusting their lives to their engineering skills, these early scientist-explorers climbed into their contraptions and sank far beneath the waves, never knowing if they'd return alive.

Where, Exactly, Is the Deep Sea?

When you wade out into the ocean, you're walking along the submerged section of the continent known as the continental shelf. Depending on where you are, the shelf may extend only a short distance or it may stretch for several hundred miles. The average continental shelf is 40 miles (64 kilometers) long. At the end of the continental shelf, the seafloor drops down along steep continental slopes to the deep ocean basin, where the geological features appear similar, though on a larger scale, to those found on land. On average, the seas in the basin are about 12,566 feet (3,830 meters) deep.

You can't put on a scuba tank and dive to the bottom of these basins, because the extreme pressure would make all of your air-filled cavities (like your lungs) instantaneously collapse. At sea level—where land is level with the ocean's surface—the air exerts 14.7 pounds of pressure over every inch of our bodies (or 1 kilogram of pressure for every 1 centimeter of skin). We

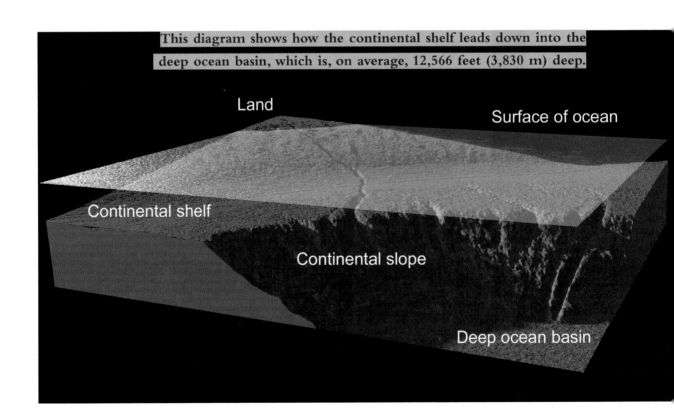

This diagram shows how the continental shelf leads down into the deep ocean basin, which is, on average, 12,566 feet (3,830 m) deep.

Land

Surface of ocean

Continental shelf

Continental slope

Deep ocean basin

don't feel it because our bodies push back in equal measure. Water, however, is about 1,000 times as dense as air at sea level. If you dive down 33 feet (10 meters), you will encounter double the amount of pressure you'd feel on the beach. If you attempted to swim 2.5 miles (4 kilometers) down to the wrecked ship *Titanic*, you'd have to be able to withstand the pressure produced by the weight of the water column above you, a feat that would be roughly equivalent to holding the Empire State Building on your shoulders!

Even sunlight can penetrate through only the uppermost 660 feet (201 meters) or so of seawater. In this region, plankton (sea plants) serve as the base of the food chain. This means that all organisms living in the surface waters depend on plankton either directly for food or indirectly by eating organisms that have eaten the plankton.

The deep sea includes everything below where sunlight dwindles at 660 feet (201 meters) and extends down to the seafloor. Since plants can't grow without sunlight, animals living in the deep sea must eat each other or the scraps that rain down from above. Different creatures live at different depths, and the farther down you go, the harsher the conditions become, which means fewer animals can exist there. The deep-seafloor itself is a largely lifeless place.

Scientists typically divide the sea into four zones. The photic zone is the shallowest, going to about 660 feet (200 meters) deep. Then the mesopelagic zone ranges from about 660 feet (200 meters) to 3,281 feet (1,000 meters) in depth. An estimated 90 percent of the creatures living in this zone are bioluminescent, which means that, like fireflies, they emit their own light. Most glow blue because this color travels best in water. They use bioluminescence for a variety of reasons, including to attract and illuminate prey, space themselves out as they hunt, find a mate,

A decapod shrimp spits out light in order to evade its predator.

avoid predators, distract predators with a light show, or attempt to
make themselves look bigger than they are.

The bathypelagic zone encompasses depths below the
mesopelagic to about 13,100 feet (4,000 meters). Fish found in
the bathypelagic regions of the deep sea are well adapted to living in an environment where food is scarce. They tend to have
big mouths, fearsome-looking teeth, and stretchy stomachs. This

allows them to gulp down a meal whole. If they took smaller bites, another predator might steal the food away and precious crumbs would drop to the seafloor.

The third zone, the hadopelagic, is very poorly studied. It encompasses water in the deep-ocean trenches, including the Mariana Trench, which plunges to a depth of nearly 7 miles or 35,810 feet (10,915 meters).

Photos taken from space show that most of our planet—71 percent—is covered with blue water. This doesn't reveal the full measure of the ocean's vastness, however. The ocean's volume makes up 99 percent of the habitable space in which life can exist. Humans and all other surface creatures dwell on a comparatively thin strip of land and air, while marine creatures swim

The anglerfish has a long stalk that snakes out of its snout or chin. At the stalk's tip, there's a glowing bioluminescent blob that it uses like a fishing pole. The anglerfish waves the glowing blob around and lures smaller fish into its vicious teeth.

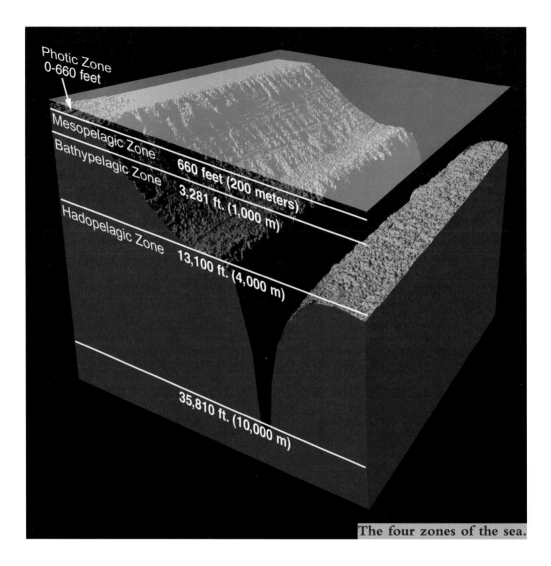

Photic Zone
0-660 feet

Mesopelagic Zone

Bathypelagic Zone

660 feet (200 meters)

3,281 ft. (1,000 m)

Hadopelagic Zone   13,100 ft. (4,000 m)

35,810 ft. (10,000 m)

The four zones of the sea.

throughout the ocean's full fluid realm. Further, the sunlit regions of our seas make up only 2 to 3 percent of the available living space, while the majority—97 percent—lies in the dark and largely unexplored regions of the deep sea.

"The potential for fundamental discoveries is high for anyone who goes into the field of deep-sea research with open eyes and an intuitive mind," said oceanographer Dr. Cindy Lee Van

Dover. "I sensed all this profoundly when I first began to think about what might lie beneath the surface of the oceans. I also felt the romantic draw of deep-sea research—sailing on the high seas, exotic port stops, a chance to prove myself against the elements."[2]

Outer versus Inner Space

Surprisingly, it's less complicated to conduct research in outer space than it is in "inner space," a term used to describe the deep sea. For astronauts, it's difficult to leave the bounds of Earth's gravity, but once they're out among the stars, they don't encounter huge pressure differences, and they don't need much power to float about or to communicate with colleagues on land. In contrast, working in deep water presents many complications. In addition to the problems of pressure, water also resists movement (for instance, it's harder to run in a swimming pool than it is on land). Radio transmissions are blocked by suspended particles, and without the Sun to warm the deep sea, it's very cold—the temperature in deep regions hovers just a few degrees above freezing. It's also, of course, pitch-black. Considering these obstacles, it's not surprising that the story of deep-sea exploration begins with the nuts and bolts of engineering. In order to plumb inner space, scientist-explorers first had to figure out how to build a craft capable of withstanding the journey.

Dr. Sylvia Earle said, "I had friends who were astronauts, including Kathy Sullivan, who was the first woman skywalking astronaut from this country. And I tease her sometimes about being an astronaut. All you have to be is the very best at what you do. But somebody else builds your spacecraft. . . . Those of us who yearn to go down in the sea, first of all, you've got to design your spacecraft. Then you have to find the money to build it, and then you have to find the money to operate it."[3]

CHAPTER

Getting Down There

In the 1920s, William Beebe, a wiry scientist with the New York Zoological Society, embarked on a study of deep-sea life around Bermuda. He used the researcher's standard tool at the time—nets. He'd drop these nets a mile (1.6 kilometers) down and then haul them back up and see what he'd caught. It was a pretty random process. One deep-sea researcher equated it to "trying to study a forest from a blimp and the forest is in a deep fog."[1] The limitations needled Beebe every time he gazed down at the tropical fish darting around Bermuda's shallow coral reefs. He decided he needed to dive down into the blackness far beyond his eyes' reach to witness firsthand how the creatures lived in their native environment.

In the 1930s, Beebe and engineer Otis Barton began collaborating on a design for the first deep-diving submersible. They called their sub a bathysphere, from the Greek words *bathy*, for "deep," and *sphere*, because it was a cast steel ball 4 feet 9 inches (1.5 meters) in diameter, much like a wrecking ball. They gave it two thick quartz windows and a cable that would tether it to a surface ship and supply it with electricity. It was designed to withstand pressure up to a half mile (0.8 kilometer) down.

Dr. William Beebe (right) and Otis Barton stand beside their invention, the first deep-diving submersible called the bathysphere.

Oxygen tanks would pump in breathable air. Carbon dioxide (the potentially toxic gas we exhale) would be absorbed and neutralized by trays of chemicals.

It's a bit hard today to put ourselves into these men's places and imagine the bravery it took to prepare to sink into a lightless world no one had ever visited before. They had no idea what

To enter the bathysphere, Barton (shown here) and Beebe slid through the narrow opening and assistants closed the steel door and bolted it in place.

creatures they might see, what dangers they might encounter. Beebe knew that if their bathysphere leaked in such a highly pressurized environment, death would come quickly. "There was no possible chance of being drowned," he wrote, "for the first few drops would have shot through flesh and bone like steel bullets."[2] Even though there aren't strong currents underwater, the ball often bounced violently up and down as the ship it was tethered to rose and fell on the surface waves. Periodically the bouncing got so bad that the men had to grasp on to the sphere's bottom to keep from getting thrown into the metal walls.

Between 1930 and 1934, the bathysphere made thirty-five dives, including one in which Beebe and Barton reached a depth of 3,028 feet (923 meters), a record that would stand for fifteen years. A poetic writer, Beebe captured his impressions in his book, *Half-Mile Down*:

> At the very deepest point we reached I deliberately took stock....There came to me at that instant a tremendous wave of emotion, a real appreciation of what was momentarily almost superhuman, cosmic, of the whole situation; our barge slowly rolling high overhead in the blazing sunlight. . . . The long cobweb of cable leading down through the spectrum to our lonely sphere, where, sealed tight, two conscious human beings sat and peered into the abyssal [deep] darkness as we dangled mid-water, isolated.[3]

Set Me Free

Beebe's bathysphere was a remarkable invention, but its dependence on a cable meant it was ripe for potentially deadly problems. What if that cable became snagged on rocks or other underwater obstacles? If it snapped, the bathysphere would be left helpless on the seafloor. Ideally, a deep-diving machine should be capable of rising and falling of its own accord.

Around 1920, before Beebe's first dives, a Swiss student at Zurich Polytechnic School named Auguste Piccard came up with exactly such a design. He reasoned that the trick would be to make the craft so buoyant it would require weights to sink. Once it reached the sea bottom, the weights could be dropped and the ship would shoot back up to the surface.

Before he could pursue such a design, Piccard became distracted by other pursuits, including conducting upper atmosphere research via hot-air balloons. After achieving a good deal of fame for these endeavors, the scientist (now with long white hair and a curling white mustache) turned his attention in the 1940s to designing the deep-sea submersible he'd envisioned as a young man. He described it as a bathyscaphe, from the Greek word *skaphos*, for "boat." Like Beebe's bathysphere, it featured a steel cabin, but the windows would be made of a new and incredibly strong product, Plexiglas.

In order to make the craft buoyant, Piccard attached chambers and filled them with 28,000 gallons (106,000 liters) of gasoline, which is lighter than seawater. To descend, tanks would fill with seawater, weighting the ship and sending it downward. When Piccard wanted to ascend, he'd drop a load of steel pellets. The gasoline's natural buoyancy would then help the ship rise.

In 1953 off the coast of Naples, Italy, Piccard and his adult son, Jacques, crawled into the bathyscaphe they'd named *Trieste*. It would be their first deep-sea descent, an attempt to go deeper than any human had ever traveled, their target being a section of the deep-seafloor 3,600 feet (1,098 meters) beneath the waves. As they sank, the Piccards watched the water change from blue to violet to black. Bioluminescent creatures lit up the darkness, making it seem like the Piccards were in the midst of a glowing blizzard.

In the sub's chambers, the gasoline was cooling with the decrease in water temperature and becoming heavier, increasing their weight and thus their speed. Soon they were plummeting too fast. Finally they crashed into the thick gray-blue mud of the sea bottom. The sub's spotlight lit up the area right around them. Peering out mud-splattered portholes, they saw nothing but apparently lifeless ooze disappearing into blackness. After a while, Auguste released the steel shot and the *Trieste* lurched upward. As they rose, the gasoline gradually warmed and became more buoyant, allowing them to pick up speed. Within forty-five minutes, they broke through the surface.

The U.S. Navy acquired the *Trieste* in 1958 and constructed a stronger cabin that would allow it to plunge into the deep ocean trenches. In 1960, Jacques Piccard and navy lieutenant Donald Walsh made history as they descended in the *Trieste* to the deepest point on Earth—the Challenger Deep, a section of the Mariana Trench 35,810 feet (10,915 meters) below the surface of the ocean.

The *Trieste* was a sturdy craft, but its huge size made it unwieldy and its propellers were capable of doing little more than inching it forward along the sea bottom. Scientists needed a

Jacques Piccard prepares the *Trieste* for a dive in 1959, after the navy acquired the sub.

machine they could maneuver, something along the lines of the submarines used by the navy, but one that would be capable of working at extreme depths.

Alvin

Two men in particular were committed to seeing this concept evolve into reality: Charles B. "Swede" Momsen Jr., the chief of undersea warfare for the Office of Naval Research, and Allyn Vine of the Woods Hole Oceanographic Institution (WHOI). Between 1963 and 1964 a submersible was constructed for WHOI. It was affectionately named *Alvin* for both Allyn Vine and the popular cartoon chipmunk.

Alvin relies on the same operating principles as the *Trieste* did: To go down, the ship is made heavy by filling a tank with seawater (known as ballast water). To go up, it is made light by releasing the water and dropping steel weights. Unlike the *Trieste*, *Alvin* is able to adjust its ballast water to become "neutrally buoyant" at the sea bottom (meaning that it doesn't float or sink; it just stays put). It has motors that propel it through the water like an underwater airplane. *Alvin*'s passengers ride in a cabin that is equipped with three portholes—two on its side and one in the floor. The sub also has a couple of hydraulic manipulator arms, one for jobs requiring brute force and the other for more delicate tasks. At the sub's squat nose, there's a science basket with various tools and temperature probes.

At first *Alvin* could dive 6,000 feet (1,829 meters), but over the years, newer and better components have been added to the little sub, so that now it would be hard to identify any original equipment. These upgrades allow *Alvin* to plunge to a maximum depth of 14,764 feet (4,500 meters). *Alvin* continues to make between 150 and 200 dives a year, and while there have been some close calls, no one has ever lost his life aboard it. Some scientists even joke that they feel safer in *Alvin* than in their cars.

Climb Aboard

Researchers who get picked to travel aboard *Alvin* specify a dive spot that they wish to pursue. *Alvin* is then strapped onto an A-frame crane on the back deck of its permanent "tender ship," the *RV Atlantis*, and transported to this location. The researchers don't need to know how to drive a sub; that's the pilot's job. However, they will be shown the operator's manual, which contains detailed instructions on everything they would need to know should something unforeseen happen to the pilot, requiring them to take over the controls.

To some people, *Alvin* looks like a fattened pig; to others, like a chewed-off cigar with a helmet. Despite its ungainly appearance, it is a sturdy little craft.

Once the *RV Atlantis* reaches its destination, nine or ten crew members congregate at the A-frame to prepare *Alvin* for launch. First the pilot climbs a ladder and descends into the sub, then the researchers follow. The round titanium door is sealed shut and a pair of skin divers climb atop *Alvin* and hold on as the crane hoists *Alvin* into the air. When the divers give the thumbs-up sign, the crane lowers the sub into the water very close to the ship's stern. As the sub bucks on the waves, the divers work quickly to unhook the rope that tethered *Alvin* to the crane. As soon as the sub is free, the divers leap into the water. They swim around *Alvin*, double-checking the motors, the hydraulic arms, and the science basket. When they are sure *Alvin* is safe and ready to go, they signal the pilot, who then opens the ballast tank. Air pressure sends a spray of water shooting in a plume as the tank begins to fill. This added water weight pulls *Alvin*'s orange top beneath the surface. The journey down to the deep sea begins.

The passenger cabin is very snug. The pilot sits on a cushioned box. The two scientist-passengers have to figure out how to make room on a bench that isn't much bigger than a bathtub. Tucked into a back corner is the standard *Alvin* lunch: sandwiches, fruit, candy, and coffee. No one drinks too much of the coffee, though, because there's no bathroom on board.

One of *Alvin*'s pilots described the descent this way: "Clear water quickly becomes aqua, then a deeper blue-green-black . . . then darker still, until there is no color left at all, only blackness. In this colorless transparency of water 1,000 meters [3,281 feet] and deeper, splashes of bioluminescent light silently pass by like shooting stars; they are the only index of motion as the submersible continues its plunge."[4]

Inside the cabin, red lights cast a diffuse glow. The instrument panel looks like a jet plane's, with a lot of dials and gauges. Every fifteen seconds the navigational system sends out a ping-pong tracking signal. The oxygen tanks whir and the carbon dioxide scrubbers grind softly. The researchers lie on their sides or stomachs, eyes trained on their portholes. Pilot Cindy Lee Van Dover said, "As the dive progresses, a penetrating damp chill invades. The cold water of the deep sea is ancient, and the chill that passes through the hull seems old, heavy, relentless."[5]

While *Alvin* is beloved by researchers today, the sub initially had to prove itself, just like any rookie. *Alvin* did so in a most dramatic fashion along an underwater mountain chain known as the mid-ocean ridge.

CHAPTER

THREE

The Mid-Ocean Ridge: You Won't Believe What's Down There!

If you took a cruise to Europe, there wouldn't be any evidence that your ship was passing right over the mid-ocean ridge, the biggest mountain chain on Earth. The tops of its peaks are so far under the waves that no one even knew this underwater mountain chain existed until the 1950s and 1960s when the U.S. Navy began creating seafloor maps using new sonar techniques. The word *sonar* is derived from "*so*und *na*vigation *r*anging." It refers to a device that sends sound waves through water and then records the return vibrations. Scientists could determine how far a wave traveled underwater according to the amount of time it took the wave to bounce back. Much to the scientists' surprise, sonar readings

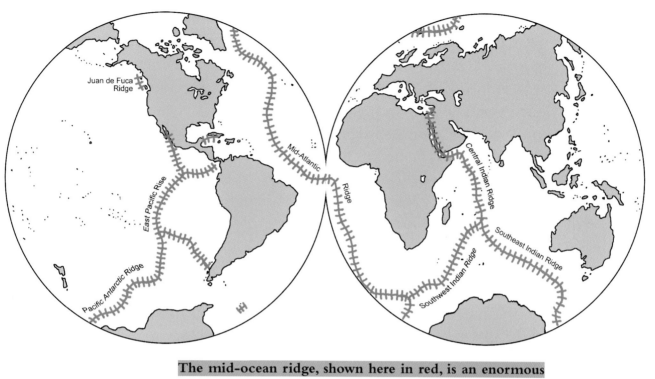

The mid-ocean ridge, shown here in red, is an enormous mountain range that encircles the planet at the bottom of the sea.

showed a massive ridge more than 35,000 miles (56,315 kilometers) long encircling the planet like a seam on a baseball.

"This mountain range covers 23 percent of the Earth's total surface area," said deep-sea researcher Dr. Robert Ballard. "Almost a quarter of our planet is one mountain range, and we didn't even know it existed in its totality until 1960."[1]

Massive Conveyor Belts

Until the discovery of the mid-ocean ridge, most scientists believed Earth's continents had remained locked in place since their formation 4.6 billion years ago. One German scientist, Alfred Wegener, bucked the trend back in 1915 when he noted

29

that similar plant and animal fossils had been found on continents separated by oceans. Furthermore, two continents in particular, Africa and South America, looked an awful lot like interlocking puzzle pieces. To explain this, he suggested that, at one time, all the continents had been part of a single landmass. Over time, the mass broke up into smaller continents that drifted apart from each other, and the oceans filled in the spaces in between—a theory Wegener called continental drift. Most of his colleagues thought he was foolish. After all, what possible force could have propelled such massive pieces of land?

The discovery of the mid-ocean ridge made continental drift seem a little less ridiculous. Geologists studying the sonar maps noted that the contours of the underwater ridge resembled volcanic zones on Earth's surface. Using huge steel nets to dredge (haul up) samples from the ridge, they found the rocks were indeed volcanic and very young. A handful of scientists suggested that the long ridge might mark a weak area in the Earth's outer layer, or crust. Perhaps two giant sections of seafloor were pulling apart and hot molten rock from inside the Earth was regularly erupting onto the seafloor—a process they dubbed seafloor spreading. In the cold deep sea, the molten rock would quickly cool and harden, forming new crust.

The scientists figured that as more molten material continued to well upward, it would push the cooler rock (or crust) farther and farther away. Indeed, dredge samples confirmed that the rock closest to the ridge (the spreading center) was the youngest and that the rock became progressively older in either direction.

Geologist Harry Hess of Princeton University envisioned the seafloor as a conveyor belt moving slabs of crust across the planet's surface. As new crust rose up at the mid-ocean ridge, it would push the older crust farther away, a force that could explain continental drift. Since new crust was constantly forming, old crust must be disappearing somewhere else. Hess thought there must be places, like deep ocean trenches, where big slabs met and one slab was driven downward (like a conveyor belt) to sink beneath the other. When the sinking slab came in contact with the Earth's hot interior, it would melt. This molten rock eventually would rise again at the mid-ocean ridge and keep the process going. The concepts of seafloor spreading and continental drift were eventually unified into a single theory called plate tectonics. According to this theory, the Earth's surface is made up of a number of crust slabs, or plates. These plates include both the continents and the seafloor. They are in constant, albeit slow, motion. Most of the boundaries between plates are under the ocean, at its ridges and trenches.

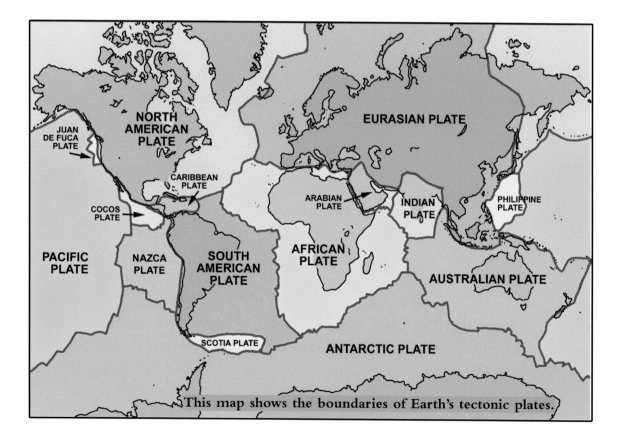

This map shows the boundaries of Earth's tectonic plates.

Hess based his ideas mainly on intuition. What little proof he had came from indirect observation—from rocks culled by dredging expeditions and by sonar mapping. Some scientists rejected the concept of seafloor spreading and insisted that the mid-ocean ridge was nothing more than a big volcanic mountain range rising out of a firmly fixed seafloor. Sure, there might be eruptions, but this was not enough to drive huge slabs of crust into motion. One scientist recalled, "It felt as if a civil war had erupted between traditional geologists and those who accepted plate tectonics. The new theory of a young, dynamic seafloor and drifting plates of crust represented a revolution as comprehensive and far reaching for the earth sciences as Newton's theory of gravity for astronomy and physics or Darwin's theory of evolution for the life sciences."[2]

The World's Most Expensive Paper Clips

In 1972 more than forty American and French scientific leaders who had been studying the mid-ocean ridge got together at Princeton University to ask the question: Do we or do we not dive to the ridge to see if seafloor spreading is occurring there? It was a lively conference to say the least, with a lot of intense debate and late-night discussions.

At this point, *Alvin* was only seven years old and had not been tested at great depths. Dr. Robert Ballard explained some of the concerns: "In the early years of the *Alvin* program there was a lot of danger. The first years of deep submergence were to de-bug it and make it work as a system, so it became routine. In the early years, there was a lot of apprehension about a deep dive: Was everything going to work? Were you going to come back?"[3]

Some conference attendees pointed out that the sub could cover only short distances. Would it gather enough important information to make it worth the high price it cost to operate? Dr. Ballard recalled that one of the most influential oceanographers of the group, Maurice Ewing, "hated *Alvin*, thought it was a silly toy. . . . The big guns were not in favor of it. . . . Ewing said to me, 'Son, . . . you may get your chance to take a submarine down into the Mid Atlantic Ridge, but if you fail, we're going to melt it down into titanium paper clips.'"[4]

Eventually, those in favor of using *Alvin* got their way. They would join France, the other global leader in deep-sea exploration, on Project FAMOUS (French-American Mid-Ocean Undersea Study). The research target was a section of ridge southwest of the Azores Islands (about 1,000 miles [1,600 kilometers] west of Portugal). In addition to *Alvin*, they'd use a French bathyscaphe and a French submersible. Each craft would focus on a particular section of the ridge. Should an emergency arise, they probably could get each other out of trouble. "Never in the history of deep submergence had so much effort gone into prepping a dive site and divers," wrote Ballard. "The preliminary work resembled the kind of planning, detailed study, simulation, and training that goes on before a major space mission."[5]

They set to work mapping the underwater section of ridge using cutting-edge sonar. The U.S. Navy donated a special waterproof camera, which the scientists towed at great depths from behind a ship to snap pictures of the ridge. They then laid out the 5,250 black-and-white photos on a gym floor. There were unweathered ridges, craggy juts, extensive lava flows running down the central valleys. (*Lava* is the term for molten rock once it has left Earth's interior.) Walking around the photos, the FAMOUS team tried to envision what they would encounter thousands of feet below the waves.

In August 1973 the French bathyscaphe began making a series of dives. The unwieldy craft spent most of its time rising and falling

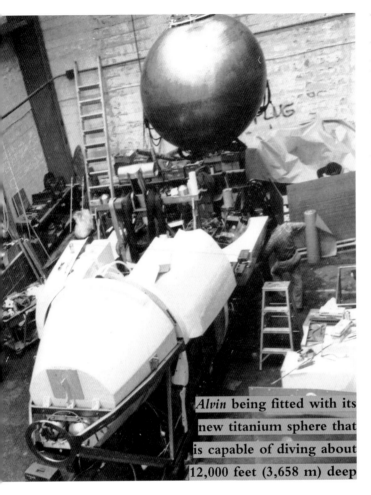

Alvin being fitted with its new titanium sphere that is capable of diving about 12,000 feet (3,658 m) deep

between lava flows, but the crews were the first humans to see first-hand evidence of fresh molten crust emerging from between two massive tectonic plates. These lava flows occurred in a valley 9,000 to 10,000 feet (2,745 to 3,050 meters) deep. At the time, *Alvin* was capable of diving only to 6,000 feet (1,829 meters). Therefore, while the French bathyscaphe was traveling down, *Alvin* was on land getting fitted with a superstrong new titanium hull, which would allow it to withstand pressures at these great depths. Finally, on June 6, 1974, the WHOI research ship *Knorr* chugged off for the mid-ocean ridge with twenty-four scientists aboard and *Alvin* strapped to the A-frame on the back of the *RV Atlantis*.

Alvin Makes a Splash

At the ridge, they met up with the French bathyscaphe and submersible. Never before had a group of deep-diving vessels carried out such an extensive research effort. Frequently all vehicles were submerged at the same time, investigating different sections of the ridge.

Dr. Ballard recalled what it was like to descend in *Alvin* to peaks that would dwarf the Andes: "You enter the mountain range, go down into this deep valley [called a rift valley], and on the floor of this valley are hundreds and hundreds of active volcanoes."[6] *Alvin's* lights illuminated pillow mounds of lava so fresh they looked like brittle black glass. Near the rift's center, the lava was slashed with deep fissures as if someone had pried the mounds apart with a spade. In fact, these fissures were caused by the frequent earthquakes that radiated out along the seafloor as the molten rock erupted and the plates shifted.

At one point, *Alvin* pilot Jack Donnelly agreed to dive into a fissure so that the scientists aboard could observe the lava layers up close. This particular fissure was a good deal wider than *Alvin*, and as the sub's lights penetrated downward, they could see no bottom. Donnelly pushed the thrusters and sent *Alvin* whizzing down and forward. The scientists eagerly began noting observations. They couldn't tell that the farther they went, the closer the

Alvin explores the Mid-Atlantic Ridge during Project FAMOUS.

Dr. Ballard supervises pilot Jack Donnelly's efforts to free *Alvin* from a seafloor fissure.

walls of the fissure pressed in on them. Suddenly they found themselves wedged in. Donnelly tried to move upward, without luck. He tried going backward and sideways, but they were stuck.

With only a limited field of vision, Donnelly gathered that they'd somehow become trapped beneath overhanging rocks. Getting on the two-way radio, he alerted his American colleagues to his predicament. They consulted the French scientific team to see if its sub could come to *Alvin*'s aid. After a brief discussion, everyone agreed that there wouldn't be much the French could do to extract *Alvin*.

"Really, there was only one choice," wrote Dr. Ballard. "Donnelly would have to try to knock his way out."[7] Pushing thrusters forward and praying for the best, Donnelly slammed the snub-nosed sub into the overhanging rocks. He gratefully noted that they broke apart. Luckily the lava was young and brittle. Before long he'd knocked open a channel and the sub began to rise again, much to everyone's relief.

In all, *Alvin* conducted seventeen dives and spent eighty-one hours on the seafloor, while the French vehicles combined to make a total of twenty-seven dives. The researchers brought back thousands of pounds of rock, water samples, and more than 100,000 photographs. Geology textbooks would need to be rewritten— plate tectonics was no longer a nutty theory. *Alvin*, too, had demonstrated its worth and silenced all talk of titanium paper clips.

CHAPTER

Discovering Hydrothermal Vents, the Jacuzzis of the Deep Sea

Given that the seafloor near the mid-ocean ridge is webbed with fissures, it's logical to assume that seawater will seep down into them. Since there's a lot of molten material lying in pockets known as magma chambers only 0.6 to 1.2 miles (1 to 2 kilometers) below the mountain ridge, this water will get superheated and become enriched with chemicals and minerals from inside the Earth. Since superhot water rises, it should make its way back toward the surface to shoot out of the seafloor in hot springs known as hydrothermal vents.

At least that's what scientists thought must be happening in the area around the mid-ocean ridge. The problem was that no

37

one on the FAMOUS expedition saw any signs of seafloor hydrothermal vent activity. If such vents didn't exist, then there must be some flaw in their understanding of heat flow, gravity, and seawater circulation. At the same time, the scientists acknowledged that they'd covered only a relatively minuscule amount of territory. Just because they hadn't found the vents didn't necessarily mean they didn't exist. It was time to mount a new search.

Instead of returning to the same area, this expedition would take place along another segment of the mid-ocean ridge, called the Galapagos Rift. Here, seafloor spreading was known to occur at a faster rate, which meant more molten material rising up from inside the Earth, allowing more heat energy to be released along this section of ridge. The scientists figured that, in an area with a lot of heat, they'd have a better chance of locating hydrothermal vents. Of course, this was assuming that such things even existed.

In the winter of 1977, *Alvin*, along with thirty deep-sea geologists and geochemists, traveled from chilly Cape Cod, Massachusetts, to the sun-splashed waters off the coast of Ecuador. Using sonar, the researchers positioned their ship, *Knorr*, over the Galapagos Rift. Rather than send *Alvin* down right away to search around blindly, they began by surveying big swatches of the ridge, hoping to detect and photograph an area with a spike in water temperature that might indicate the presence of a seafloor vent. To do this, they trailed a camera sled known as ANGUS (which stands for Acoustically Navigated Geophysical Underwater System) behind the ship at a depth of nearly 9,000 feet (2,745 meters). Encased in a steel cage, ANGUS was designed to withstand occasional crashes into underwater geologic features. Unofficially, ANGUS was nicknamed "Dope on a Rope" because of its sturdy resilience and its lack of delicate sensors. But it did have a finely tuned thermometer that would tell them if they hit a pocket of water that was even the tiniest bit warmer than the surrounding ocean.

Starting on the morning of February 15 and working straight through the evening, the scientists towed ANGUS in a weaving pattern over the Galapagos Rift valley. Depending on how the underwater geology changed, they'd haul in cable or let it out. "Down one!" the depth watcher would call to the cable's operator if he noted the sea bottom sloping downward. "Up two!" he'd call a moment later if ANGUS got perilously close to a rising cliff.

Other scientists in the ship's lab watched the temperature readings that ANGUS recorded as it moved along. They hoped for a spike, but the temperature stayed steady. This became monotonous pretty fast. Eating popcorn, downing cups of coffee, and listening to music, the scientists fought off boredom. Finally, around midnight, they hit a spike. The water temperature near the seafloor had shot up. It stayed elevated for three minutes as the ship chugged ahead, and then returned to a chilly 35.6°F (2°C). They marked the spot and continued working.

ANGUS was used to photograph the seafloor and detect any changes in water temperature.

When ANGUS ran out of film after taking 3,000 color photos, they hauled it up and took the film to the ship's processing lab. The photos showed a barren lava seafloor. When they got to the photos taken where they'd hit a spike in temperature, the scientists gasped. Here were thirteen frames showing clusters of clamshells!

"Nothing could have prepared us for what ANGUS had photographed," recalled Ballard, "one and a half miles beneath the surface . . . hundreds of clams clustered in a small area on the lava floor of the rift—thriving as if they were in an environment no more hostile than a sunny mudflat on the New England coast. We couldn't help but wonder what these large clams were doing in such numbers at that depth, in that eternal darkness."[1]

Everyone had always assumed that there were very few creatures living on the deep-sea floor. Bottom-dwellers had to toler-

These are some of the live clams that were found on the seafloor.

ate the extreme pressure and freezing temperatures. The creatures would have very little to eat. They would have to hunt down other deep-dwelling animals (of which there were few) or rely on excrement, mucus, bacteria, dead organisms, and other debris that rained down from above—known as "marine snow." Certainly no one had ever expected to find a thriving clam community. Perhaps the clamshells were the remnants of a shipboard party that had been tossed overboard as garbage? But no, studying the photos, the scientists concluded the clams were alive. That was certainly odd. Shoving the coordinates for the site into his back pocket, pilot Jack Donnelly, along with geologists Jack Corliss and Tjeerd van Andel, climbed into *Alvin* to investigate.

Where Are the Biologists When You Really Need Them?

As Alvin approached the target coordinates, the sub's temperature sensor started beeping. The water was getting hotter and turning cloudy blue from minerals. Here were the vents they'd hoped to find!

"We can actually see [hot] water shimmering out of cracks immediately below us," said Dr. Corliss into his tape recorder. "We're going to try to stick a probe into it now. The bottom temperature we have . . . is very erratic. A range of about a tenth of a degree, it's going up and down."[2] As they moved on, the scientists spotted the clams.

"We've arrived at what looks like a clambake," announced Dr. Corliss. "They're shells." He laughed with delighted disbelief. "They're big, uh, shells. . . . There are some living ones here, attached shellfish. . . . They look about six inches [15 centimeters] long. They grow on pillow basalt." A few moments later he reported, "We're stopped on the clambake area, maneuvering to sample some. There are clams, crabs, both live and dead, shells and

It was quite a shock to scientists when they found unknown creatures such as tiny crabs and tube worms living at the bottom of the sea.

some puffy looking things. . . . What are those sort of puffball things floating around? That's amazing. That's a big clam!"[3] And by big, he meant *really* big—the deep-sea clam was more than a foot (30 cm) in length, while most clams are about the size of your palm or smaller. And that wasn't all. *Alvin*'s lights illuminated lobsterlike creatures, shrimp, crabs, small pink fish, bizarre animals that looked like dandelions gone to seed, and odd worms with red heads that protruded from white tubes. These became known as tube worms.

Listening to the men's excitement via audiophone, the crew on board the *Knorr* stared at one another, perplexed. Did anyone know such creatures existed? There wasn't a deep-sea biologist on board to help them. They got on the CB and called up Woods Hole Oceanographic Institution, one of the finest marine research facilities in the world.

Giant clams? Weird tube worms? No, the Woods Hole biologists had neither seen nor heard of such creatures.

Until this time, life in the seas and on the Earth's surface was thought to be ultimately dependent on the ability of green plants (including plankton in the oceans) to convert sunlight and carbon dioxide into food, a process known as photosynthesis. But here, far from where light could penetrate, thrived colonies of never-before-seen creatures.

Over the course of the next few days, the scientists used ANGUS to target other shimmering hydrothermal vent locations. "What is so remarkable," said Dr. van Andel after completing a series of dives, "is that each vent seems to have a different colony of organisms around it, depending on the temperature of the hot water. We've seen scores if not hundreds of animals. . . . The mollusks and other filter-feeding organisms cling to the rocks right around the warmth; the fish lie there with blessed expressions on their faces, obviously enjoying themselves."[4]

Everyone started jockeying for a chance to ride down to the vents in *Alvin*. Instead of collecting rocks as planned, they collected creatures. "Literally every organism that came up was something that was unknown to science up until that time. It made it terribly exciting. Anything that came up on that basket was a new discovery," said Dr. Richard Lutz.[5]

Stinky Food

Obviously these creatures had to be feeding on something plentiful, but what? A clue came when the chemists aboard the *Knorr* opened a vial of vent water that instantly filled the room with the stench of rotten eggs. Gagging, people rushed to throw open the lab's windows. That particular stink could only belong to one thing—a chemical called hydrogen sulfide. When the chemists studied the stinky water under a microscope, they saw it swarmed with one-celled organisms known as microbes. How and why were these microbes living in hot vent water pouring out from inside the Earth?

They began to suspect that they'd discovered a new realm of life. "I think," said Dr. Corliss, "what we are finding will prove to be the greatest discovery in the history of benthic [sea bottom] biology."[6]

Here, 9,000 feet (2,745 meters) down, microbes were ingesting the vent chemicals, including the usually toxic hydrogen sulfide, and converting those chemicals into energy, a process the scientists called chemosynthesis. These microbes, in turn, were being eaten by larger vent creatures. It was an amazing discovery. This was a totally new type of food chain thriving in one of the most extreme environments imaginable. Equally amazing was the realization that some of these microbes, particularly those found in the hottest areas, were a genetically ancient type of organism, perhaps the most ancient on Earth.

A New Kind of Eden?

Before vent microbes were discovered, many scientists believed that life on the planet began when either sunlight or a lightning bolt simmered chemicals in a shallow pond, inducing chemical reactions that would eventually create the building blocks of life. The theory proposed that, over time, life evolved to survive in harsher regions such as the deep sea.

In 1983, however, Dr. Jack Corliss and some colleagues wrote a paper suggesting that life might instead have originated at deep-sea vents. He proposed that 4 billion years ago, these microbes began to "eat" the chemicals surrounding them. It wouldn't be until about 2.5 billion years ago that microbes evolved to use sunlight to photosynthesize. Instead of life beginning on the Earth's surface and moving downward into the deep, life might have begun in the deep oceans and worked its way upward toward land.

It's reasonable to assume that, if life could have evolved in the deep oceans, perhaps it could also have evolved in other extreme locations out in the universe, such as on Europa, the volcanically active moon that orbits the planet Jupiter and apparently has an ocean under an ice cover. Until we manage to travel to Europa's surface, we will not know if life exists there or not. However, one thing is clear: Should the Sun ever disappear or the climate grow too harsh to sustain life on the surface of the Earth, the vent microbes will still be able to exist in their pitch-black chemical world. The giant clams and dandelions will probably still be there ingesting the percolating microbes, and the tube worms will continue waving their weird red heads.

Living Lipsticks

As soon as biologists heard about the vent creatures, they could not wait to go investigate. Other expeditions were mounted to find new vents. Biologists began to carefully catalog the creatures and often dissect them to try to learn as much as possible about their organs and life systems. One journalist who helped out on a tube worm dissection said, "Cutting open the tube is the easy part. It's picking up and measuring the soft red worm that's inside that was a challenge for me. I felt I held a creature from another planet."[7] A deep-sea biology graduate student who helped the journalist explained that you don't always have to cut the worm out, you can sometimes just squeeze the tube. "Like deep sea toothpaste," she said, and pressed the tube flat at one end.[8] *Plop*, the worm shot out onto the table.

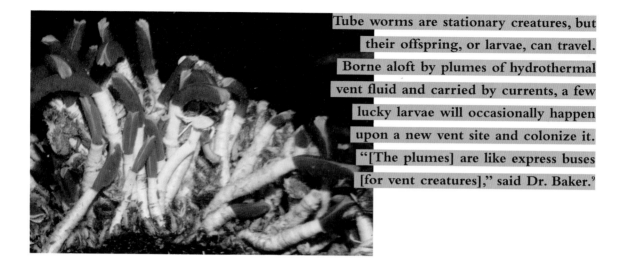

Tube worms are stationary creatures, but their offspring, or larvae, can travel. Borne aloft by plumes of hydrothermal vent fluid and carried by currents, a few lucky larvae will occasionally happen upon a new vent site and colonize it. "[The plumes] are like express buses [for vent creatures]," said Dr. Baker.[9]

Remarkably, when you dissect a tube worm, you won't find a mouth, stomach, or any other hint of a digestive tract like most other worms possess. Instead, there is an odd branching yellow organ. This organ is packed full with living chemosynthesizing microbes that convert vent chemicals into energy. The worm uses this energy to survive. In return, the worm's red gills keep a steady supply of raw materials flowing to the microbes inside it. This I'll-help-you-if-you-help-me arrangement is called a symbiotic relationship.

Biologists Dr. Charles Fisher and Dr. Richard Lutz have found that tube worms can grow up to 32 feet (10 meters) in length at rates of almost 3.2 feet (1 meter) a year, making the worms the fastest growing of all known marine invertebrates (animals without backbones). "They live hard, live fast, and die young," joked Dr. Fisher.[10] It's an important strategy when you consider the tube worm's environment is equally short-lived—most vents last only a year or two before their plumbing systems clog and shut off the water flow.

In addition to the weird creatures, there was something else unexpected about the vents—their plumbing ran cooler than anticipated. The highest water temperature noted by the scientists in 1977 was a tepid 73°F (23°C). Lab tests, however, showed that at one time, the water had boiled at between 660°F and 750°F (349°C and 399°C), probably when it was near a magma chamber. Clearly the water must have traveled some distance in order to cool this much. Were there vents, the scientists wondered, closer to magma chambers where scalding water shot straight out into the deep sea? "Would such eruptions be fairly continuous?" Dr. Ballard asked. "Somehow it seemed unlikely. In theory it might be possible, but in practice we found it difficult to find even tepid water, let alone hot."[11] Scientists did eventually locate such eruptions of hazardously hot water and found themselves contending with a lot more danger than they had bargained for.

Danger: Black Smoker Ahead!

In the spring of 1979, a team of scientists converged on yet another spreading center, known as the East Pacific Rise, off the coast of Mexico. Their goal was to conduct numerous geological experiments, including ones designed to locate magma chambers under the seafloor.

On April 21, WHOI's Dudley Foster piloted *Alvin* down beneath the waves to the coordinates of a brand-new vent site discovered by ANGUS. He saw clams, although they all appeared to be dead, and the water was cloudier than usual, a swirling gray. Suddenly up ahead, a huge chimneylike formation loomed. A dense black cloud billowed from its top. As Foster moved in for a closer view, something felt wrong with the controls. A current was pulling him toward the "black smoker." It seemed that the chimney was sucking in water, and *Alvin* was caught in that current. The portholes turned black in a cloud of thick particles. Foster was flying blind and crashed into the chimney. It toppled over, breaking at the base.

Black smokers come in all shapes and sizes—some are pointy cone-shaped structures and others branch like candelabras. Some have large appendages sticking out of their sides that hold upside-down pools of hot water, like inverted bathtubs.

Breaking the chimney helped lessen the current. Now the cloud poured out from a much larger opening, losing its sucking power. Foster heaved a sigh of relief and lowered the sub down to the seafloor, once again fully in control. All around him broken chimneys littered the ground. Using *Alvin*'s manipulator arm, he took a temperature probe from the science tray. Holding the T-shaped crosspiece at its top, he shoved the probe into the smokelike cloud puffing from the chimney's broken base. The temperature reading shot up. When he shoved it farther down into the hole, the temperature was off the 212°F (100°C) scale. As he removed the probe, Foster saw that it had melted. Dropping weights, he hastily backed *Alvin* away.

Back on board the research ship *Knorr*, scientists took one look at the mangled probe and ran for their laptop computers. They researched the melting point of the plastic material and found it was 356°F (180°C)! Pacing around *Alvin* on the tender ship's deck, Foster felt a shiver pass through him. He'd been very lucky indeed—a part of the sub's hull had melted!

On the next trip down, scientists used a probe capable of withstanding higher temperatures and discovered that the vent water was surging out at 662°F (350°C). Normally such superheated water would turn to steam, but they found that, in the deep's tremendous pressures, it stays a shimmering liquid. When this liquid cools in the sea, the minerals it has gathered from inside the Earth precipitate, or form into, particles. As the minerals accumulate, a chimney starts to build up from the ocean floor.

A journalist who hitched a ride aboard *Alvin* described approaching a chimney in this way: "It was getting murkier and murkier. . . . [The chimney] materialized slowly out of the gloom before us, increasingly clear as we moved forward through the murky water. The chimney was poised on the fissure's rim. It was a patchwork of dark and light colors, framed by the dark surrounding lava. Its bottom was thick and craggy, perhaps ten or twelve feet [3 or 4 m] across. Its midsection slowly tapered upward, like a spire. The image of the monolith overflowed my monitor as we drew closer. . . . The craggy tower was spewing water that shimmered with motion."[12]

The discovery of superhot vents helped scientists finally answer an important question: Why is the sea salty? For years, it

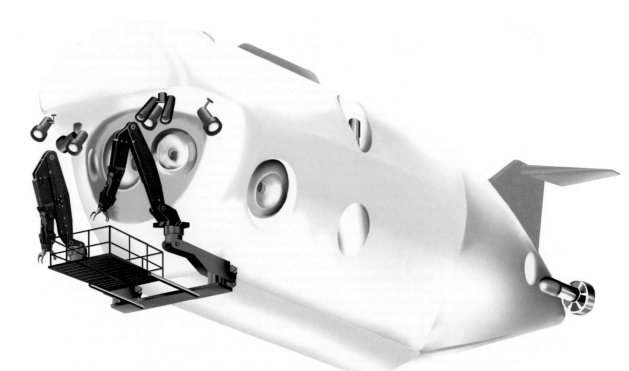

This is an illustration of a new sub being built by Woods Hole Oceanographic Institution that will eventually replace *Alvin* and will be capable of diving more than 20,000 feet (6,096 m) deep.

was known that some salt comes from the global river system, but not enough to account for the sea's composition. Now scientists understood that seawater picks up the rest of its minerals as it cycles through the Earth's hot lower crust and rises through vents. In fact, it appears that all the world's oceans filter through deep-sea ridges and vents once every 8 million to 10 million years.

CHAPTER

Exploring the Glowing Water

In the 1970s, deep-sea biologist Dr. Bruce Robison (known to just about everyone as Robey) went on numerous dives in *Alvin*. With each trip, he became increasingly fascinated by the bioluminescence flashing outside the portholes as the sub sank and rose through the waters of the mesopelagic region. He desperately wanted to stop en route and investigate. *Alvin*, however, was designed to take scientists from the surface down to the sea bottom and back up again; it was not made to hover in the water column in between. To try to learn about the creatures living in that water column, Robey had to rely on nets, just like his predecessor William Beebe had. From on board a surface ship, he'd drop these nets to a specific depth, close them, and then haul them back to the surface. "Marine biology," grumbled one of his colleagues, "is the only science still using 150-year-old technology."[1]

Any biologist investigating an ecosystem wants to know how the food chain works—who eats whom. For this reason, the fish and squid that Robey caught ended up on his dissection table so he could analyze their stomach contents. Over time, however, he and a couple of his colleagues began to suspect that the creatures trapped in these nets turned on each other in unnatural ways, falling into feeding frenzies that would never occur in nature. To test this theory, they filled their nets with chopped up rubber bands and styrofoam cups. When they pulled up the nets, they found the creatures had ingested these alien objects. Robey knew he had to find a better way to investigate the mesopelagic realm firsthand and see how the creatures behave in their natural environment. "Oceanography is a science that is best conducted by being on the ocean, being in it, and being surrounded by it," he said. "There is no substitute for direct, real-time, at sea experience. As Jimmy Buffett sings, 'don't try to describe the ocean if you've never seen it.'"[2]

Robey Gets His Wish

Finally in 1985, technology caught up with Robey's ambitions. Graham Hawkes, owner of Deep Ocean Engineering, designed a sub capable of zipping around the mesopelagic region like a helicopter. The single-passenger *Deep Rover* is an acrylic sphere with motors on the bottom. Best of all, its controls are simple enough to allow a scientist to serve as pilot. "If you can drive a car, you can 'fly' the *Deep Rover*," asserted Graham Hawkes.[3]

His codesigner, Dr. Sylvia Earle, explained, "If you want to go forward, you simply slide your arms forward a little bit. And

Graham Hawkes working on his plans for the *Deep Rover* in 1983

Marine biologist Sylvia Earle and engineer Graham Hawkes, the brain trust behind Deep Ocean Engineering, edit underwater film footage.

microswitches under the arm rests kick in, engaging the thrusters, and forward you go. You want to go in reverse, you slide your arms back a little bit. If you want to dive, press down with your wrists, the vertical thrusters are engaged, and down you go."[4]

The sub was also incredibly mobile. As one journalist who rode in *Deep Rover* enthused, "It glides forward with surprising grace. I can make it spin on its axis, or execute sweeping curves, or tip to one side. . . . We swoop, the sub and I, we twist and gambol."[5]

Thrilled by *Deep Rover*'s potential, Robey used every penny of a $250,000 National Science Foundation grant to lease the sub for a month's worth of dives into the deep waters off Monterey Bay, California, in the summer of 1985. Before each dive, Robey would get settled in the sub's armchair. The crew would crank the

Deep Rover must be secured with seven tag lines because the ship's movement could cause the sub to swing dangerously.

In *Deep Rover*, Robey bobs on the surface of the water for a few minutes, double-checking for leaks before descending.

two halves of the bubble together and bolt them shut. A crane lifted the sub into the water, then it would begin its plunge to 2,000 feet (610 meters) below the waves.

Describing Robey's trip, Dr. Earle said, "To be able to go down, along those beautiful [underwater canyon] drop-offs, and to see the change in life as light diminishes, finally into blackness. . . . It's a marvelous experience. It's a thrill at every turn. It's an opportunity for discovery of the sort that we must have if we are to understand how the ocean really works."[6]

Deep-Sea Goo

Suspended motionless, Robey marveled at the bioluminescent animals floating around his acrylic sphere. As he nudged the sub forward, he stimulated them to glow. A fish's blue inner organs flashed on and off. A long eel-like creature whizzed past like an indigo flare.

In addition to fish and eels, a stunning number of jellyfish and other gelatinous creatures surrounded Robey. He realized that these jellies were so fragile, they would've disintegrated if caught in one of his sampling nets. This was the previously indefinable goo he'd seen covering the fish and eels he'd caught in his nets. "I was amazed. . . . ," he said later. "Just using nets, we've missed about one-third of the animals in the ocean."[7]

One of the most remarkable jellies Robey captured on film was a siphonophore, which seems to be a chain of little jellyfish strung together. It was a mass of bellies, mouths, and tentacles. Today, researchers think that the colony acts as one organism with some jellies supplying stomachs, others doing the work of swim-

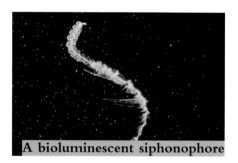
A bioluminescent siphonophore

ming, and some killing for food. Growing to a length of 160 feet (49 meters) or more, siphonophores consume so much food that they compete with big carnivores like sharks and whales. Dr. Robison approached one of these massive creatures and brushed it with his sphere. The touch caused the creature to light up, piece by piece, and glow for a full minute!

Robey wondered what other animals, including giant squid, might lurk just out of sight, frightened by *Deep Rover*'s presence. "You go to depth, trim out to neutral buoyancy, and shut everything down, no lights, no sound. . . . [With night-vision goggles] I could see the wakes of relatively large animals in close to the sub. When I kick on the lights, I'd see something taking off. I'm convinced that there are a large number . . . of fast moving, agile critters there, avoiding our present-day instruments, but I think [in the future] we can make . . . the instruments less obtrusive and investigate that further."[8]

Eye-in-the-Sea

One scientist attempting to do this is Dr. Edie Widder of Harbor Branch Oceanographic Institution (HBOI). In 2001 she engineered the Eye-in-the-Sea stealth camera system. What makes this camera so special is that it can sit on a tripod on the seafloor for a day or two filming the creatures that come into view. The camera produces an infrared glow that most sea creatures cannot detect, yet provides adequate light for capturing photos.

On its first deployment on July 23, 2002, in Monterey Canyon, California, Eye-in-the-Sea leaked and the water damaged the power supply. On a second test, off the coast of South Carolina in August 2002, the camera's internal computer crashed. The camera was retrieved, and, working on the research vessel, Dr. Widder tried to repair it. She worked all day and by evening reported, "The patient isn't looking too healthy at the moment, but I haven't given up hope. I have a saying posted over my desk back on land. . . . 'Success in life depends on how well you handle Plan B. Anyone can handle Plan A.'"[9] Despite the problems, Dr. Widder did manage to fix the camera and took a few deep-sea images. They came out fuzzy, but the important thing was that the creatures seemed unaware that they were being filmed. In the future, Dr. Widder hopes to get enough government funding to iron out the kinks for additional deployments.

Dr. Edie Widder prepares her Eye-in-the-Sea camera system before sending it down to the seafloor.

Deep-Sea Robots

Robey's *Deep Rover* success led scientists to push for remotely operated vehicles (ROVs) capable of conducting more comprehensive surveys of the mesopelagic region. ROVs are cheaper to use than submersibles and, unlike humans, can stay underwater for days at a time. One such ROV, *Ventana*, built and operated by the Monterey Bay Aquarium Research Institute (MBARI), looks like a *Star Wars* android, with its propellers, mechanical arms and hands, and suction tubes. An orange tether connects *Ventana* to the mother ship where pilots in a control booth direct its movements in water up to 6,200 feet (1,890 meters) deep. *Ventana*'s hands are extremely precise and quite strong: "I can take a penny out of your hand," said Knute Brekke, MBARI senior pilot, "and then I can fold the penny in half."[10]

Before a typical launch, technicians run through a thorough system check. Sitting on deck, the robot starts to move, its propellers hum, the arms swing around, lights turn on and off. When it has been cleared for send-off, a crane lifts *Ventana* into the water, where its thrusters churn up the water as it speeds away from the ship. Then, like a massive sea creature, it plunges out of sight.

Down in the mother ship's darkened control room, scientists gather around the monitors that project almost in real time what *Ventana*'s cameras film. Bathed in bluish light, the chief pilot sits before a joystick that allows him to maneuver the ROV.

When *Ventana* approaches an animal, the scientists ask the pilot to stop and zero in. Lasers allow them to identify the size of an animal, something that can be hard to do when you're looking at an image on a video screen. Sometimes they have the pilot use the suction tube to capture the animal so they can study it up close.

A diver prepares the remotely operated vehicle *Ventana* for its descent.

Quite often *Ventana* videotapes creatures no one has ever seen before. For example, on March 31, 2003, during a trip to the Gulf of California, Robey reported, "Today's dive started out as a snoozer.... Eventually things began to pick up, and we were glad we had the videotape running after all. For all of us who were in the control room, this dive will forever be defined as the one where we found that funny squid. And funny is just the right word because pilots and scientists alike were giggling, and then laughing the whole time it was on screen.... It doesn't fit the description of any species covered in the literature we have with us.... It is being called the Rastafarian, pig-nosed, helicopter-tailed, hippo-squid, depending on who you ask of course."[11]

This is the funny-looking squid that was discovered by *Ventana*'s camera. It is one of many unknown creatures that *Ventana* has discovered.

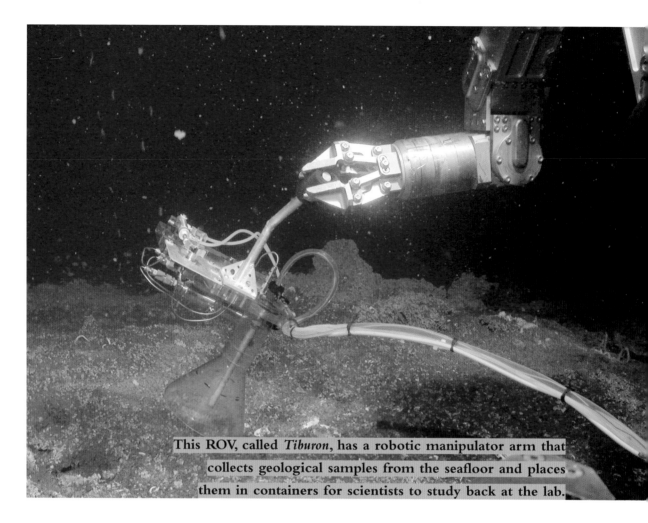

This ROV, called *Tiburon*, has a robotic manipulator arm that collects geological samples from the seafloor and places them in containers for scientists to study back at the lab.

In addition to discovering new creatures and looking into the secret lives of octopuses and squid, *Ventana* is proving very useful in helping scientists unravel the deep-sea food chain. An important link in this chain was discovered when *Ventana* tracked a creature now known as a larvacean. This tadpolelike animal is about the size of a shelled peanut and constructs a complex mucus web up to 6 feet (1.8 meters) wide to catch food and debris falling through the water. These webs have an inner mesh filter that allows the creature to pick out edible microscopic particles. When the mucus web gets clogged with excessive debris, it collapses with its own weight and sinks very quickly, carrying a rich, nutrient-laden web down to the seafloor, providing food for the creatures down there. "We all thought, and taught, that nutrients reached the ocean floor as a fine rain of sediments," said Robey. "For decades we knew the deep sea ocean floor was using more food than could be accounted for, and now, here we have an unaccounted for transport mechanism for getting nutrients to the ocean floor."[12]

ROV investigations have also shown that a number of mesopelagic creatures, especially jellies, travel thousands of feet up and down the water column every day, feeding in shallower water at night and returning to the darker depths during the day. Deep-sea biologists speculate that this may be the largest mass migration of animals on Earth.

It is humbling to think of all the other creatures living so close to us that no one has yet seen. Some scientists estimate that there may be as many as 10 million species in the deep sea, most of them unidentified. As dimensionless and unexplored as the ocean may seem, scientists are beginning to understand the density and distribution of animals living in its deepest reaches. They look forward to going deeper, staying longer, and learning more in the future.

While studying the deep sea is not a simple task under any conditions, it is arguably hardest in an ocean covered with floes of perpetual ice. And yet, in 1999, a team of scientists did just that.

CHAPTER SIX

Arctic Adventure

In May 1999 geologist Dr. Margo Edwards prepared to leave her Hawaiian home and head north. Her destination: a rugged base camp set up on the Arctic ice. She would spend the night there before boarding a U.S. Navy nuclear submarine to serve as the head scientist on an expedition known as SCICEX (Science Ice Exercise) '99, which was to map and sample the Arctic seafloor.

"The primary reason for my trip to the Arctic," Edwards wrote, "was to learn about Earth's climate. That's an odd statement if you consider the source: I'm a geologist who specializes in mapping the seafloor. What could the seafloor in the Arctic possibly have to do with global climate? The answer is 'a lot.'"[1]

In the 1990s scientists noted that balmy waters from the Atlantic Ocean had pushed into the Arctic Basin, raising the average temperature of the surface water from near freezing to as much as 35°F (2°C). This warmer water was melting sections of the Arctic ice pack and reducing what's known as the reflective layer.

Snow-white ice reflects the Sun's rays back into space, while exposed dark water absorbs the warming rays. The more water that's exposed, the warmer that water will get. Looking into the future, scientists could imagine that the warmer water might eventually melt most or all of the ice pack. If this happened, it would not directly cause a disastrous rise in sea level, but it could speed up a process known as global warming.

Global warming refers to the rise in the Earth's surface temperature, which increased by about one degree Fahrenheit during the last century. Many scientists believe that humans, through pollution, are altering the Earth's climate. If the Arctic ice pack melted, it could help increase global temperatures. This would cause glaciers to melt, raising the water level of our oceans. Land currently at sea level would be underwater—say good-bye to places like New York City, Lisbon, and Tokyo.

BRRR!

Dr. Edwards landed in Point Barrow, Alaska, the last stop before she reached the Arctic. "I get off the plane in an Aloha shirt and a fleece jacket," she recalled with a laugh. "I ran as quickly as I could across the tarmac into the [terminal] building and waited, desperate, for my down jacket to get unloaded."[2]

A week earlier, her colleagues had scouted out a location for the SCICEX base camp. Using a small Cessna plane, they scanned the white landscape for a section of ice that might be thick enough to hold the scientists and their equipment. When they spotted a contender, they touched down and then quickly took off again. Circling back around, they checked to see if any new cracks had appeared. When they found a place that didn't show cracks, they figured the ice was sufficiently thick. Landing again, they kept the plane's engine running, just in case, and jumped out with a big corkscrew to drill down and confirm the ice's thickness. Once they'd located a good spot, they started hauling in equipment and setting up the camp so that the rotating teams of SCICEX scientists would have a place to stay before and after their stints on the submarine. Not surprisingly, a lot of planning goes into building an Arctic base camp. "You can't run down to the hardware store or the electronics shop," said Peter Mikhalevsky, a scientist at the camp. "It's all got to be right there."[3]

This is the base camp of SCICEX '99. The bright yellow shacks and tents are called hooches.

Hooches

As Dr. Edwards flew into the base camp, she noted that it looked like a little plywood shack village. The surrounding landscape was more beautiful than she'd imagined. "It's not at all flat," she said softly, "there's these huge pressure ridges with hills. There are places called 'leads' where the ice is broken and you can see the very dark water. The most interesting thing was that it's a very musical place. You could hear the humming of your footsteps. I'd been to snowy places, but not frozen places like this, so I was blown away."[4]

She was also blown away by the extreme cold. The temperature hovered between −10°F and −20°F (−23°C and −29°C). With wind, it would get even colder. The hooches were equipped with butane heaters. Because heat rises, the bottom bunk would be freezing and the top bunk sweltering. Being from Hawaii, Edwards of course picked the top bunk. But there was no way to avoid the cold when, in the middle of the night, she needed to leave the cozy hooch and venture across the ice to the unheated outhouse with its frosty toilet seat!

The next morning, Edwards and the rest of the crew ate a big breakfast cooked by the camp's chef and then headed across the ice to meet the submarine. A nuclear sub can do things no surface ship can—it isn't impeded by ice or storms and doesn't need to refuel often. It is also very stable and quiet, which makes it good for conducting sonar mapping of the seafloor.

This sub had traveled underwater all the way from Hawaii and was scheduled to break through a section of weaker ice not too far away. As the scientists set out hiking, they realized a lead had opened up in the night. They laid a toboggan over this weak patch to act as a bridge. Stepping onto the toboggan, Edwards felt it bob beneath her boots, an unsettling experience.

Crashing Through the Ice

Ideally, when surfacing, a sub rises straight up with zero angle, so that its sail (the stovepipelike section above the main body) thrusts straight through the ice ceiling. Inside the sub, the skipper counts down the meters until impact and the crew feels surprisingly little. On the surface, it's an awesome sight. "When the submarine was coming up," Edwards said, "it was like a big bubble forming under the ice and there's a loud crack and the ice you're standing on starts to bob."[5] When the sail broke through, the scientists cheered.

Edwards's friend, Dr. Mark Rongstad, had been aboard the sub and asked if she would take him for a quick tour of the ice camp. Instead of using the toboggan bridge, Rongstad thought he saw a better place to cross. As he stepped forward, the ice cracked. He plunged down into the 34°F (1°C) water.

The navy's nuclear submarine USS *Hawkbill* broke through the ice at the SCICEX camp. The sailors, who had been underwater for weeks, eagerly threw open the hatch and jumped out. They needed to take some time to walk around and breathe fresh air.

"We were probably 200 yards from the sub," said Edwards, "And I'm signaling to them. They're contacting ice camp to come and get us."[6] Perhaps thinking he'd try to get out on the other side, Rongstad paddled around. Edwards couldn't believe he'd turned his back on her as if discounting her ability to help him. "When he did that I got really mad," she admitted. "I thought, 'He thinks I'm a girl and I can't handle this.' So I reached down and he had this video camera strap across his shoulder and chest, and I grabbed him. Of course you don't have any traction because you're on the ice and it's wet, but I managed to get him out of there. If he hadn't turned his back on me, I think I would've kept on panicking. . . . I found out later Mark was wearing a wet suit [under his clothes] which is why he stayed so calm. But in an instant," Edwards said, "it went from 'Oh, this is very exciting,' to 'Oh my God, my friend could've died.'"[7]

Although badly shaken, Edwards knew she had to keep her wits about her and get ready to work. For months she'd been preparing for her week aboard the sub. While most deep-sea research projects conducted from surface vessels have about 30 crew and 15 scientists, SCICEX '99 had 130 crew and 5 scientists. It was also about ten times as expensive as most research ventures, which meant that not a minute could be wasted. Edwards had carefully choreographed the trip to ensure they got the maximum possible work done. There was no time to dwell on what might've happened to Mark Rongstad if he hadn't been wearing a wet suit.

All Aboard!

Edwards entered the sub via a hatch behind the sail. The top level was the command area and periscope room. Down in a lower level, the navy had converted a section of the torpedo room into

Dr. Edwards briefs the crew members and scientists on board the *Hawkbill*.

a research station. It looked like a long hallway with equipment at one end and cots for thirty sailors to sleep there. In this room, Edwards stood (since there wasn't room for a chair) and monitored a special sonar system called SCAMP (Seafloor Characterization And Mapping Pod).

SCAMP would send out sound waves as the sub traveled. The returning echoes mapped the seafloor in two different ways. One map showed the height of objects on the seafloor while another map showed the objects' texture. Edwards compares it to using two maps to understand your own neighborhood. You might have an aerial photograph that shows the layout of houses and streets, but you wouldn't know if those houses and streets were on hills or valleys, so you'd need another map to give you a sense of the rise and fall of the landscape. Taken together, the two maps will give you a good idea of the actual place where you live. Similarly, the two sonar maps told Edwards a lot about what the deep-sea terrain looked like. "Never before had anyone gathered this level of detail about the Arctic floor," she said.[8]

While Edwards studied SCAMP, the navy used its own sonar to negotiate through the Arctic waters. At one point, the submarine appeared to be heading straight for a big cliff. Electronics Technician 3rd Class Tommy Erikson was on watch and notified the officer of the deck that it looked like they were on a collision course. The crew sounded the alarm. "Red sounding" blared through the sub and everyone braced for the crash . . . that never came.

Downstairs in the torpedo room, Edwards was watching her own sonar and could see the bottom far away from them. "I think they tracked a false echo," she said.[9] To understand how this can happen, imagine shouting "hello!" across the Grand Canyon. A lot of echoes will bounce back to you. It's the same with a sub's sonar. It sends out a note and gets a lot of echoes back. Sometimes the sonar can get hooked not on the first echo, as it's supposed to, but on the second or subsequent echoes, so that it seems like the seafloor is doing something it isn't. Edwards suspects that while the sailor changed the paper in his sonar machine, it started tracking the wrong echo. When the captain ordered the crew to steer the large sub back around and investigate, they found that there was, indeed, nothing there.

Massive Glaciers

Edwards and her colleagues were still digging through data from the expedition years later, but the biggest finding so far is that the Arctic basin is scarred by deep tracks. At some point in the past, a really big piece of ice, 0.6 miles (1 kilometer) thick, scratched the seafloor as it moved along. The implications are far-reaching. Edwards says the models scientists had been using to understand global warming were based on the assumption that the Arctic ice had always maintained its current thickness. Now those global warming models have to be revised to take into account a period of time when the Arctic ice was much thicker. This, she says, will improve scientists' ability to understand the climate in the past and help predict how it might or might not change in the future.

"It's kind of like the stock market," she explained. "If we know that every so many years there's a spike when everyone sells, we can predict what will happen in the future. . . . Knowing that the ice was thick at a different point in time can now be added to the climate models. . . . It can help answer the question: Are people contributing to global warming? Better baseline data of what happened in the past will give us a better idea of whether or not people are affecting the climate now."[10]

Like most deep-sea researchers, Edwards considers her trip beneath the surface a life-altering experience. "It taught me that I still know how to have faith that things beyond my control will work out for the best . . . that people with varied backgrounds, beliefs, and interests can come together to do something remarkable for the whole world."[11]

As scientist-explorers continue to harness ever better technologies to probe the deep's mysteries, it is easy to forget how far this field has come in such a short time. In a book recounting her trips to the deep-seafloor, Dr. Cindy Lee Van Dover wrote, "What still seems remarkable to me is that less than twenty years ago we could not even imagine the existence of hydrothermal vent communities, and we knew next to nothing about the biota [life] that wanders the abyssal [deep sea] plains. We landed a man on the moon nearly a decade before we ever saw the heat of our own ocean's crust exhaled through black smokers. . . . There has never been a more exciting time to be a deep sea scientist, and I for one celebrate the fact that the abyssal wilderness is modest neither in measure nor in mystery."[12]

Glossary of Terms

bathypelagic: The waters of the deep sea ranging from depths of about 3,281 feet (1,000 meters) to about 13,100 feet (4,000 meters).

bathyscaphe: A very pressure-resistant deep-diving machine that can rise and sink on its own but otherwise has extremely limited mobility.

bathysphere: The spherical diving bell constructed by William Beebe in the 1930s.

bioluminescence: The ability some creatures possess to produce their own light through biochemical reactions. Many deep-sea creatures are bioluminescent.

black smoker: A seafloor chimney composed of the minerals that accumulate around superhot hydrothermal vents; it has hot, black, mineral-laden fluid shooting out of it.

chemosynthesis: The process by which microbes convert chemicals into energy. Microbes found at hydrothermal vents rely on this to survive.

continental drift: The process of the Earth's large crustal plates slowly drifting in relation to each other, carrying continents with them.

continental shelf: The submerged section of the continent.

crust: The Earth's outer surface.

deep sea: All the ocean's water that extends from where sunlight dwindles, at about 660 feet (201 meters) down, to the seafloor and bottoms of the ocean trenches.

extremophiles: Microbes and other organisms that live in environments that would be extreme and hostile to humans. For example, all the creatures living at deep-sea hydrothermal vents.

hadopelagic: The deep-sea waters below 13,100 feet (4,000 meters) down to the bottom of the deepest ocean trench, 35,810 feet (10,915 meters).

hydrogen sulfide: A chemical, toxic to humans, that chemosynthesizing microbes ingest and then convert into energy.

hydrothermal vent: A mineral-rich seafloor geyser created when seawater seeps into cracks in the Earth, gets heated by molten rock, and rises back to the surface.

invertebrates: Animals without backbones.

larvacean: A deep-sea creature that makes a mucus web to catch edible particles. When the web becomes too heavy, it sinks to the seafloor, providing bottom-dwellers with an important source of nutrients.

lava: Molten rock once it has erupted onto the Earth's surface.

magma: Molten rock beneath the Earth's surface.

magma chamber: Reservoir of molten rock beneath the Earth's surface, including along the mid-ocean ridge.

marine snow: The constant, very slow rain of mucus, bacteria, and the remains of gelatinous creatures that sinks through the water column and provides some nutrition for deep-sea animals.

mesopelagic: The waters of the deep sea ranging from depths of about 660 feet (200 meters) to 3,281 feet (1,000 meters).

plate tectonics: The geological theory that posits that the surface of the Earth is made up of large plates that are in constant slow motion.

reflective layer: This refers to the way the Arctic's snow reflects Sun rays back into space.

ROV: Stands for remotely operated vehicles, which scientists use to study the deep sea.

seafloor spreading: The phenomenon occurring along the mid-ocean ridge where two tectonic plates pull apart allowing molten rock to rise up from inside the Earth and erupt on the seafloor. As the spreading continues, the cooler rock is pushed farther and farther away.

siphonophore: A bioluminescent deep-sea creature comprised of many individual jellies that have bonded together to act as a single organism.

submersible: The term for a science submarine; it is smaller and deeper-diving than a military submarine.

symbiotic relationship: This refers to a mutually beneficial relationship between two organisms—an I'll-help-you-and-you'll-help-me partnership. For example, the tube worms and vent microbes that live within them.

Source Notes

Introduction: Meet a Deep-Sea Scientist

1. Maria Puente, "Testing Waters to Learn More About Giant Squid." [Online] Available at www.ncf.carleton.ca/~bz050/HomePage.usasquid.html, May 14, 2003.
2. Laura Allen, "Stalking the Giant Squid," *Science World*, November 3, 1997, p. 11.
3. Arthur Fisher, "He Seeks the Giant Squid." [Online] Available at www.seawifs.gsfc.nasa.gov/OCEAN_PLANET/HTML/ps_roper.html, June 4, 2003.
4. Craig Pittman, "The Calamari Safari." [Online] Available at augustachronicle.com/stories/053000/tec_UE0183-6.shtml, January 26, 2005.
5. Pittman.
6. Bijal P. Trivedi, "Giant Squid Washes Ashore in Tasmania." [Online] Available at www.news.nationalgeographic.com/news/2002/07/0726_020726_L psquid.htm, May 14, 2003.

Chapter One: The Unknown Deep

1. Richard Ellis, *Deep Atlantic: Life, Death, and Exploration in the Abyss* (New York: Alfred A. Knopf, 1996), p. 86.
2. Cindy Lee Van Dover, *The Octopus's Garden: Hydrothermal Vents and Other Mysteries of the Deep Sea* (Reading, MA: Addison-Wesley Publishing Company, 1996), p. 5.
3. Jill Wolfson, "An Interview with Sylvia Earle." [Online] Available at http://www.thetech.org/revolutionaries/earle/, June 8, 2003.

Chapter Two: Getting Down There

1. Shannon Brownlee, "Explorers of Dark Frontiers," *Discover*, February 1986, p. 61.
2. Robert D. Ballard and Will Hively, *The Eternal Darkness: A Personal History of Deep-Sea Exploration* (Princeton, NJ: Princeton University Press, 2000), p. 9.
3. Edward H. Shenton, *Diving for Science: The Story of the Deep Submersible* (New York: W.W. Norton, 1972), p. 47.
4. Cindy Lee Van Dover, *The Octopus's Garden: Hydrothermal Vents and Other*

Mysteries of the Deep Sea (Reading, MA: Addison-Wesley Publishing Company, 1996), p. 32.

5. Van Dover, p. 33.

Chapter Three: The Mid-Ocean Ridge: You Won't Believe What's Down There!

1. "The Hall of Science and Exploration: Robert D. Ballard, Ph.D." [Online] Available at www.achievement.org/autodoc/page/bal0int-1York, June 4, 2003.

2. Robert D. Ballard and Will Hively, *The Eternal Darkness: A Personal History of Deep-Sea Exploration* (Princeton, NJ: Princeton University Press, 2000), pp. 124–125.

3. "The Hall of Science and Exploration: Robert D. Ballard, Ph.D."

4. Woods Hole Oceanographic Institution, "The Discovery of Hydrothermal Vents 25th Anniversary: Interviews: Robert Ballard." [Online] Available at www.divediscover.whoi.edu/vent_cd/site_index.html, June 6, 2003.

5. Ballard and Hively, p. 129.

6. "The Hall of Science and Exploration: Robert D. Ballard, Ph.D."

7. Ballard and Hively, p. 161.

Chapter Four: Discovering Hydrothermal Vents, the Jacuzzis of the Deep Sea

1. Robert D. Ballard, "Notes on a Major Oceanographic Find," *Oceanus*, Summer 1977, p. 75.

2. Woods Hole Oceanographic Institution, "The Discovery of Hydrothermal Vents, 25th Anniversary: The Trail of Discovery: Jack Corliss Makes his First Observations of the Clambake Area." [Online] Available at www.divediscover.whoi.edu/vent_cd/site_index.html, June 6, 2003.

3. Woods Hole Oceanographic Institution, "The Discovery of Hydrothermal Vents, 25th Anniversary: The Trail of Discovery: Jack Corliss Makes his First Observations of the Clambake Area."

4. Woods Hole Oceanographic Institution, "The Discovery of Hydrothermal Vents, 25th Anniversary: The Trail of Discovery: Spring 1979, Oases of Life." [Online] Available at www.divediscover.whoi.edu/vent_cd/site_index.html, June 6, 2003.

5. Woods Hole Oceanographic Institution, "The Discovery of Hydrothermal Vents, 25th Anniversary: The Trail of Discovery: Spring 1979, Oases of Life."

6. NOAA, "Ocean Explorer: Explorations: Galapagos Rift." [Online] Available at oceanexplorer.noaa.gov/explorations/02galapagos/background /history/history.html, June 1, 2003.

7. Joanna Lott, "Fourth Dispatch: Worm Science." [Online] Available at www.rps.psu.edu/deep/dispatch04.html, June 4, 2003.

8. Lott.

9. John Fischman, "In Search of the Elusive Megaplume." [Online] Available at www.findarticles.com/cf_0/m1511/3_20/54359915/p1/article.jhtml?term= +In+search+of+elusive+megaplume, June 4, 2003.

10. John Travis, "Live Long and Prosper," *Science News*, September 28, 1996, p. 201.

11. Robert D. Ballard and Will Hively, *The Eternal Darkness: A Personal History of Deep-Sea Exploration* (Princeton, NJ: Princeton University Press, 2000), p. 195.

12. William J. Broad, *The Universe Below: Discovering the Secrets of the Deep Sea* (New York: Simon and Schuster, 1997), pp. 139–140.

Chapter Five: Exploring the Glowing Water

1. Asee Prism Online, "Briefings: Faulty Flotation Devices, Snapping Sea Species, Having a Ball: Deep Sea Digital." [Online] Available at www.asee.org/prism/jan02/briefings.cfm, June 16, 2003.

2. MBARI: Gulf of California Expedition, February 19 – May 30, "Researchers." [Online] Available at www.mbari.org/expeditions/GOC /researchers/Leg3.htm#Bruce%20Robison, November 24, 2003.

3. Hi-Q Products, Inc., "Deep Rover Submersible." [Online] Available at www.hiqproducts.com/rover.html, June 12, 2003.

4. "The Hall of Science and Exploration: Sylvia Earle: Ph.D. Interview." [Online] Available at www.achievement.org/autodoc/page/ear0int-5, June 12, 2003.

5. Shannon Brownlee, "Explorers of Dark Frontiers," *Discover*, February 1986, p. 61.

6. "The Hall of Science and Exploration: Sylvia Earle: Ph.D. Interview."

7. Bijal P. Trivedi, "Underwater Robot Tracks Elusive Jellyfish." [Online] Available at www.news.nationalgeograph…/news/2003/01/0117_030117_ tvjellyfish.html, April 25, 2003.

8. Access Excellence @ the national health museum, "BioForum for High School Science Teachers: Advances in Deep Sea Biology." [Online] Available at www.accessexcellence.org/BF/bf03/panel/bf03.html, November 24, 2003.

9. NOAA, "Ocean Explorer: Explorations: Islands in the Stream: Logs: August 23, 2002." [Online] Available at www.oceanexplorer.noaa.gov/explorations /02sab/logs/aug23/aug23.html, June 12, 2003.

10. Dennis Moran, "Gathering the Bay's Mysteries." [Online] Available at www.montereyherald.com/mld/montereyherald/5146991.htm, January 26, 2005.

11. MBARI: Gulf of California Expedition, February 19 – May 30, "Logbook: March 31, 2003." [Online] Available at www.mbari.org/expeditions/GOC /logbook/Leg3/Mar31.html, June 12, 2003.

12. Trivedi.

Chapter Six: Arctic Adventure

1. Margo Edwards, "The Science of SCICEX." [Online] Available at www.cnn.com/SPECIALS/2001/icerun/scientist/, June 4, 2003.

2. Margo Edwards, personal interview, March 26, 2003.

3. Douglas S. Wood, "The Ultimate Camping Trip." [Online] Available at edition.cnn.com/SPECIALS/2001/icerun/living.arctic, March 24, 2003.

4. Edwards, personal interview.

5. Edwards, personal interview.

6. Edwards, personal interview.

7. Edwards, personal interview.

8. Edwards, personal interview.

9. Edwards, personal interview.

10. Edwards, personal interview.

11. CNN.Com: In-Depth, "Ice Run: Submarine to the Arctic." [Online] Available at www.cnn.com/SPECIALS/2001/icerun/, November 24, 2003.

12. Cindy Lee Van Dover, *The Octopus's Garden: Hydrothermal Vents and Other Mysteries of the Deep Sea* (Reading, MA: Addison-Wesley Publishing Company, 1996), p. 72.

Further Information

If you feel driven to tackle the deep's challenge, you'll first need to arm yourself with a good foundation in one of the related sciences, like oceanography, biology, chemistry, and/or geology. In high school, take as many science classes as you can. At college, you'll first need to get a bachelor of science degree and then go on to get a Ph.D. As a graduate student, you will probably have the opportunity to join a deep-sea expedition and maybe even dive in *Alvin* or another submersible. In the meantime, you can learn more about the deep sea by looking into some of the resources that follow.

Books

Ballard, Robert D., and Will Hively. *Eternal Darkness: A Personal History of Deep-Sea Exploration*. Trenton, NJ: Princeton University Press, 2002.

Ballard, Robert D., and Malcolm McConnell. *Adventures in Ocean Exploration: From the Discovery of the Titanic to the Search for Noah's Flood*. Washington: National Geographic, 2001.

Beebe, William. *Half a Mile Down*. New York: Harcourt, Brace & Company, 1934.

Broad, William J. *The Universe Below: Discovering the Secrets of the Deep Sea*. New York: Touchstone Books, 1998.

Byatt, Andrew, et al. *Blue Planet*. London: DK Publishing, 2002.

Earle, Sylvia. *Atlas of the Ocean*. Washington: National Geographic, 2001.

Ellis, Richard. *Deep Atlantic: Life, Death, and Exploration in the Abyss*. New York: Knopf, 1996.

Ellis, Richard. *The Search for the Giant Squid*. New York: Penguin Books, 1999.

Hoyt, Erich. *Creatures of the Deep*. Westport, CT: Firefly Books, 2001.

Jefferis, David. *Megatech: Super Subs: Exploring the Deep Sea*. New York: Crabtree Publishers, 2001.

Kunzig, Robert. *Mapping the Deep: The Extraordinary Story of Ocean Science*. New York: W.W. Norton & Company, 2000.

Rice, A. L., and Tony Rice. *The Natural World: The Deep Ocean.* Washington: Smithsonian Institution Press, 2000.

Robison, Bruce. *Monterey Bay Aquarium Natural History: The Deep Sea.* Monterey Bay, CA: Monterey Bay Aquarium Foundation, 1999.

Van Dover, Cindy Lee. *Deep Ocean Journeys: Discovering New Life at the Bottom of the Sea.* Cambridge, MA: Perseus Publishing, 1997.

Van Dover, Cindy Lee. *The Octopus's Garden: Hydrothermal Vents and Other Mysteries of the Deep Sea.* Reading, MA: Addison-Wesley Publishing Company, 1996.

Vanstrum, Glenn. *The Saltwater Wilderness.* New York: Oxford University Press, 2003.

Videos

The Blue Planet: Seas of Life. London: BBC Video, 2002.

Great Minds of Science: Oceanography. New York: Unapix, 1997.

NOVA: Into the Abyss. Boston: WGBH, 1998.

Sea Monsters: Search for Giant Squid. Washington: National Geographic, 1998.

Web Sites

ALVIN Simulation and Training: www.whoi.edu/marops/vehicles/alvin/alvinsim/index.html

Dive and Discover: Expeditions to the Seafloor: www.divediscover.whoi.edu/

Extreme 2002: Mission to the Abyss: www.ocean.udel.edu/extreme2002/home.html

Giant Squid Links: www.mysteries-megasite.com/main/bigsearch/squid.html

Harbor Branch Oceanographic @ Sea: Exploring the Ocean Frontier: www.at-sea.org/default.html

Harbor Branch Oceanographic: Fathoming the Gulf Stream: Secret Lights in the Sea (streaming video): www.at-sea.org/missions/fathoming/biolum.html

Harbor Branch Oceanographic Web site: www.hboi.edu/index_03.html

HURL: Hawaii Undersea Research Laboratory:
www.soest.hawaii.edu/HURL/hurl.html

In Search of Giant Squid: seawifs.gsfc.nasa.gov/squid.html

Links for Biological Oceanography: www.geology.ucdavis.edu/~sumner
/Teaching/GEL116f00/116biolinks.html

Monterey Bay Aquarium Research Institute: Cruise into the Classroom: Gulf of
California Expedition: www.mbari.org/expeditions/goc/index.htm

National Geographic: Kaikoura Canyon Dispatches (Giant Squid Search):
www.nationalgeographic.com/kaikoura/index.html

National Oceanic and Atmospheric Administration Ocean Explorer Explorations:
www.oceanexplorer.noaa.gov/

New Millennium Observatory: A Seafloor Observatory at an Active Underwater
Volcano: www.pmel.noaa.gov/vents/nemo/

NOVA: Into the Abyss: www.pbs.org/wgbh/nova/abyss/

The Ocean Conservancy: www.oceanconservancy.org/

Savage Seas: The Deep Sea: www.pbs.org/wnet/savageseas/deep-main.html

SCICEX-99: Undersea Science at the Top of the World:
www.chinfo.navy.mil/navpalib/cno/n87/usw/issue_4/scicex_99.html

Smithsonian Ocean Planet Plunge Video (from outer space to inner space):
seawifs.gsfc.nasa.gov/OCEAN_PLANET/HTML/oceanography_flyby.html

Smithsonian: Ocean Planet Resource Room:
seawifs.gsfc.nasa.gov/OCEAN_PLANET/HTML/ocean_planet_resource
_room.html

Smithsonian: Ocean Planet Simulated Trip Along Sea Floor:
seawifs.gsfc.nasa.gov/OCEAN_PLANET/VRML/k30_vrml2.wrl

Woods Hole Oceanographic Institution: The Discovery of Hydrothermal Vents,
25th Anniversary: www.divediscover.whoi.edu/vent_cd/index.htm

Index

Page numbers in *italics* refer to illustrations.